Caring for Box

SAGE
PRESS

Published in 2003

SAGE PRESS,
PO Box Nº 1, Rye, East Sussex TN36 6HN.
e.mail: sagepress.bm@btinternet.com
www.sagepress.co.uk
Text © Lynn R. Batdorf
Illustrations © Sage Press 2003
RHS Update © Dr B Henricot

Set in Palatine italic 9 on 11 point leading.
Display in Palatino Bold Italic 14 point.

Design and Illustrations
Chris Monk of Yellowduck Design & Illustration.

Text
Lynn R. Batdorf

Editor and Publisher
Mrs Bobby Meyer

Printed in England

ISBN: 0-9542297-4-6.

🐚 Caring for Box

Contents

❧ Caring for Box

PUBLISHER'S FOREWORD

When I first read Lynn Batdorf's article on 'Effective Cultural Techniques to prevent and control Boxwood Diseases', which appeared in the Summer 2001 issue of Topiarus - the magazine for members of the European Boxwood and Topiary Society (EBTS*) - I had just planted a long-planned small box parterre. I mixed both mature cones and balls I had bought in Belgium, which had moved with me on a number of occasions, and new hedging plants sourced in the UK. Having dreamt of this project for many years I was very concerned to do all I could to make it a success and found myself referring to Lynn's article time and time again.

It was packed with essential information needed by enthusiasts and growers and, seeing how useful it was in helping me care for my own box, it dawned on me that this text would make an ideal companion title to BOX, one of the very first titles to be published in the Sage Press 'Collector's Series of Trees'.

Many readers of BOX have told me personally how much they enjoy and use this little book and I sincerely hope that CARING FOR BOX will find an equally valued place on their bookshelf or even in the potting shed.

I have tried to do everything Lynn recommends to help me stay free of the dreaded box blight which has sadly hit many established box gardens. Readers will be encouraged to read in the RHS Update on page 26, kindly contributed by Dr. Beatrice Henricot, that the RHS is working hard to identify fungicides to control the current diseases. And in the last few days only I have learnt that Amistar, an agricultural fungicide not available to the general public, can be used as a preventative measure. I am told that it is effective in keeping the disease at bay and seems to stop it spreading if spraying is accompanied by good box hygiene as described by Lynn Batdorf.

Treatment includes cutting back the diseased box branches to the main stem and takes a strong heart. But I know from a friend whose lovely box garden has been severely affected that the treatment does work. I should add that Langley Boxwood Nursery (see advert on inside front cover) provide a spraying service to clients in the South East of England.

I am very grateful to Lynn Batdorf for his generosity in granting Sage Press permission to reproduce his article as text for CARING FOR BOX and also wish to thank Dr. Beatrice Henricot for her contribution updating us on the important work she and her team are carrying out at the RHS to help us overcome the devastating effects of box blight.

Mrs. Bobby Meyer
Publisher Sage Press   *Beckley, March 2003*

* see p 28 for further details of EBTS

❧ Caring for Box

Why Grow Box?

Box is tolerant of most soils and a wide array of climatic conditions, thrives in shade or sun, and has a diversity of forms, from a dwarf to tree-like. Deer and other wildlife do not feed on boxwood, making it useful in rural and suburban landscapes. Its hard wood makes it a durable ornamental shrub that can live for centuries. Applying appropriate cultural techniques for boxwood will greatly increase its vigour and allow it to reach its full potential in the landscape. Proper cultural techniques can also deter diseases and can reduce or eliminate damage if present.

Maintaining a Disease Free Plant

A healthy boxwood requires proper site conditions as one of its most important considerations.

Optimum soil pH is a critical factor which is easy to correct, but is often overlooked. A soil pH between 6.5 and 7.2 allows the proper soil nutrients to be available for boxwood. If the pH is below the recommended range, add dolomitic lime. The rate is dependent upon existing soil pH and soil type. Dolomitic lime is preferred since it can buffer the soil pH for several years. An ideal soil is loamy with balanced portions of sand, silt, and clay. Competition for water and nutrients from the roots of nearby trees, shrubs, and turf grass should be avoided.

Remember the Roots

The roots of boxwood reach out at least to the drip line, of the outermost boxwood leaves, and most will grow beyond that. The majority of boxwood roots are near the soil surface, and this feature becomes important in watering, fertilizing, mulching and transplanting boxwood.

Optimal site conditions should offer protection from sunshine and wind during the winter months. Some boxwood exposed to continuous direct sun in winter develop discoloured leaves due to rapid temperature changes. Windy sites in winter will cause the boxwood to lose water faster than it can be absorbed by the roots. Boxwood planted with exposure to the south or west during the winter months is predisposed to winter bronzing. Boxwood is tolerant of shade and full sun, but performs best in partial sun. Those in full sun are often troubled by mite damage and leaf scorch, as well as winter discolouration and damage. The loss of chlorophyll (green pigments) exposes carotenoids (red and orange pigments) and causes the orange or reddish-brown discolouration of the leaves. Boxwood in full shade has reduced vigour and sparse foliage due to lower light levels.

Cultural Stress

Boxwood, like most living organisms, is subject to stress. A plant can be stressed by biotic conditions such as pests, diseases and weeds or by abiotic conditions, such as water and temperature extremes. Foliage bronzing in late fall and early spring, small leaves and heavy fruiting are typical symptoms of cultural stress.

Pruning

Thinning is the single most important maintenance activity for keeping Buxus sempervirens 'Suffruticosa' healthy. The majority of its foliage growth is at or near the ends of the branches, resulting in a dense outer shell of foliage with only a few leaves in the centre. Thinning is a type of pruning that reduces this thick, terminal foliage. Overly thick terminal foliage results in inadequate light and air circulation through the interior of the plant. Under these conditions, the interior leaf shoots die, leaving very little green foliage on the majority of the branch.

Different Approaches to Pruning

In Europe, B. sempervirens 'Suffruticosa', when used in parterres or as edging plants, is sheared regularly to maintain symmetry and keep it small and tight. Such artificial manipulation creates a highly stressed plant. Shearing encourages dense branching and leaves are cut into pieces. In addition, 'Suffruticosa' typically grows to 8' (2.4 m) or more. When constantly sheared to maintain a height of 1' or 2' (30 cm to 60 cm) it is subjected to long-term, low level stress.

Boxwood normally maintains a leaf for three years. The carbohydrates produced by the leaf over the three years replenish important food reserves within the plant. When a leaf is sheared off after a few months, after it is fully developed the plant is deprived of a portion of the carbohydrates it needs and is slowly starved.

Pruning and topiary work, creates a
beautiful boxwood specimen, but
subjects the plant to chronic stress.
This eventually weakens the boxwood,
making it susceptible to disease.
Thinning is an important corrective
action for this condition.

All About Thinning

To thin B. sempervirens 'Suffruticosa', small branches about 6" to 8" (15 cm to 20 cm) in length are randomly removed from the most dense portions of the plant.

If the interior branches are not visible, the foliage is too thick and must be thinned. Preferably, thinning should be done annually, but it must be done at least every two years. The best time to do the thinning is late November through December. In addition to this being the best time of year for the plant, the cuttings can be used for holiday decorations.

Fertilising

There is no regular schedule for fertilizing boxwood. The most reliable indicator for when, how much, and what type of fertilizer is a soil test. A proper soil analysis will indicate fertilizer needs for a specific site. Leaf colour may also be a clue to inadequate nutrient levels. If the boxwood begins to show symptoms of nitrogen deficiency, for example, it may be time to fertilize.

Spotting the need to fertilise

The earliest symptom of nitrogen deficiency is yellowing of lower or interior leaves. The plant will have a rather uniform yellowing that is more pronounced on the older, interior leaves. As the deficiency becomes more acute, the leaves become smaller and thinner and turn quite bronze in winter. Boxwood leaves should remain on the plant for three years; if they fall off earlier, this may be a sign of nitrogen deficiency. Granular, urea fertilizer with a 10-6-4, or similar, analysis is appropriate in most situations. Late fall applications of fertilizer promote root growth and provide the best results.

When and How to Fertilise

Boxwood should not be fertilised in the spring since this encourages foliage growth that is not balanced by proper root development. The fertiliser should be applied by broadcasting it around the base of the shrub to just beyond the drip line. Surface application is the easiest, fastest and most effective technique. It is particularly effective when applied near the drip line since the most active roots are located in that area.

As the soil pH decreases below 6.0, the magnesium becomes less available resulting in the foliage discoloration seen here. Maintaining a soil pH between 6.5 and 7.2 ensures maximum nutrient availability.

The Advantages of Mulching

Mulch is critical to maintaining healthy boxwood, performing many beneficial functions. It conserves soil moisture by reducing evaporation from the soil surface and reduces weed growth. Mulch aids water penetration into the soil, slows the full force of heavy rains, and reduces the danger of soil erosion. Soil temperature is moderated since the mulch, acting as an insulator, reduces temperature fluctuations. The soil remains cooler in the summer, which encourages root growth. In the winter the soil is not as likely to alternately freeze and thaw, which may injure the roots near the surface. Soil fertility is increased as nutrients and organic matter become available as the mulch decomposes. Finally, certain mulches improve the overall appearance of the garden.

Preferred Mulches for Box

There are several materials that can be used to mulch boxwood: shredded hardwood bark, hardwood chips, geotextile fabric, compost and shredded leaves. Materials that do not make good mulch for boxwood are: pine bark, sawdust, peat moss, stone chips, gravel, and plastic. Mulch should be applied only to a depth of 1" (2.5 cm). If the mulch is being used to top dress existing mulch, remove some of the existing mulch and apply only enough to bring the total depth to 1" (2.5 cm). Avoid mounding mulch under branches to discourage adventitious rooting. Over a period of time the organic materials used in mulch decompose adding humus and plant nutrients to the soil. As this occurs, it will be necessary to add additional mulch to maintain the 1" (2.5 cm) mulch depth.

Sanitation

Maintaining a clean environment is critical in maintaining healthy boxwood, especially for Buxus sempervirens 'Suffruticosa'. The incidence of disease, pest damage, and abnormal growth can be avoided by proper sanitation techniques. Once a year the leaves and twigs that have accumulated in the centre of the boxwood ought to be cleaned out. A strategy that includes thinning the foliage, followed by shaking the branches and raking up the debris, gives the best results. First, thin the plant to reduce the dense foliage and prune out dead twigs. After pruning is completed, a vigorous shaking of the branches will force the debris to fall to the ground. Finally, a leaf rake can be used to collect the debris which should then be removed from the site. Periodic cleaning improves the air circulation and sunlight in the interior of the plant. It also removes much of the inoculum available to propagate fungal diseases.

Fungal diseases

Poor air circulation promotes the fungal diseases Macrophoma leaf spot, Volutella leaf and twig blight, and Cylindrocladium. In addition, the branches become thin and weak, making them more susceptible to breakage from snow and ice. Thinning allows the centre of the plant to receive enough sunlight to grow interior foliage and stronger branches. Thinning also allows air to freely circulate through the interior of the plant reducing and even eliminating fungal diseases. Indeed, the decline of English boxwood and its susceptibility to fungal diseases is the direct result of overly thick foliage.

Disease

Fungi are responsible for more plant diseases than any other group of organisms and cause most of the diseases in boxwood. Fungi are small, generally microscopic in size, with a plant-like body. Since fungi lack chlorophyll, they spend at least part of their lives taking food from host plants or from dead plant material.

Keeping boxwood healthy greatly reduces their susceptibility to disease. By properly selecting a boxwood cultivar, placing it in the appropriate site and properly caring for it, the impact of disease can be reduced or eliminated.

The important aspect of managing disease is to avoid the initial infection. This is accomplished by proper culture which has already been discussed. If disease avoidance is unsuccessful, then correct

Healthy Box plant showing its small, greenish flowers set in clusters of both male and female in the leaf axils

diagnosis at the important early signs is required to avoid the spread and propagation of the disease. Unfortunately, the early signs of disease are all too often overlooked or not understood. Once the disease has been diagnosed, prompt corrective measures will give the most effective results.

The important fungal diseases of boxwood can be grouped into two categories; the first two diseases affect the roots and the other affect the foliage or twigs. Both produce symptoms that appear on the foliage.

Phytophthora

Phytophthora *means plant destroyer, which gives an indication of how serious this problem can be. There are about 40 species, but only one,* Phytophthora parasitica, *is important to boxwood. This soil-borne fungus affects all cultivars of* B. sempervirens *at any age or size. It damages the roots of boxwood growing in wet or poorly drained soils. Infection is common in the spring and fall when the soil is wet and cool, about 58º F to 70º F (15º C to 21º C). The disease progresses and causes injury only under higher soil temperatures. Damage occurs at 75º F (24º C), with the greatest effects occurring at 85º F (30º C). As a consequence of root loss, the leaves gradually turn yellow then change to a bright straw colour and remain attached to the twigs. This may happen to one branch, or several, or throughout the entire shrub. Boxwood infected with* Phytophthora *seldom survive. Because* Phytophthora *produces spores that move in a water film, the best strategy to avoid this disease is to plant boxwood only in a well-drained soil.*

Symptoms of the disease include roots and stems with vascular tissue that has turned a dark brownish-black colour. Check under the bark near ground level. The bark may be decayed and is easy to remove. The fungus causes a partial, or even complete, blockage of nutrient and water movement in the stem. The roots appear dull and dark brown in colour. This is in contrast to healthy bright, light tan roots.

Nematodes

Nematodes, small eel-like worms, can also harm boxwood. They live as an obligate parasite, one that can only grow and multiply when on a living host. However, they can survive as an egg or cyst for several years without the benefit of a host. Living in the soil, nematodes feed on the roots of boxwood. The first visible symptoms are wilting, stunting, and yellowing or bronzing of the foliage. If boxwood are growing in proper cultural conditions and exhibit these symptoms, then nematodes are suspect. The only reliable method of determining the presence of nematodes is to collect soil and root samples from a suspect boxwood and have the sample examined by a plant nematologist.

Lesion or meadow nematodes, Pratylenchus *spp.*, are very destructive to B. sempervirens cultivars and B. microphylla *var.* japonica. These nematodes prefer to feed on the smallest roots; this has a root-pruning effect, which may be followed by root rot from a secondary infestation of pathogens. Above-ground damage is slow to appear, but results in smaller leaves that are yellow or, more often, reddish. The foliage may shed prematurely, retaining

Nematode damage results in damaged roots which reduces the ability of the boxwood to produce and maintain leaves.

only one or two years of foliage. Root knot nematodes,
Meloidogyne spp., *cause swelling of the roots. The formation
of a gall stops root growth, reducing the availability of
nutrients and water. The plant will be stunted with short
shoots, and small yellowish or bronze-coloured leaves.*

*Nematodes cannot be totally eliminated from the soil.
The goal is to keep the population low enough to prevent*

damaging symptoms that weaken the plant. Boxwood should not be grown in soils heavily infested with nematodes. In the long term, growing plants such as grasses that are not affected by nematodes will reduce nematode populations. A biological control, Bacillus penetrans, *has been effective in treating the soil for root knot nematodes. However, this control option for* Pratylenchus *is either not effective or practical in the landscape.*

Macrophoma

A disease affecting the leaf, Macrophoma leaf spot or Macrophoma candollei, is an imperfect fungus that limits itself to Buxus sempervirens *'Suffruticosa'. Macrophoma is saprophytic only and comes in after other diseases, winter injury, or other events that can cause cultural stress. If present, the pycnidia, round and hollow fruiting bodies appear as tiny, black, raised spots on the underside of either the light green or, more commonly, tan-coloured foliage. The large, transparent, single-celled conidia are produced in large quantities and ooze out of the pycnidium when placed in water. Water is the primary means of dispersal and movement for fungi. The fruiting bodies first appear on the oldest leaves inside the centre of the plant. As the infestation progresses, it affects the younger leaves and causes defoliation. Heavy infestations can cause entire branches to die in only a few weeks.*

Typically Macrophoma leaf spot can be corrected by pruning out the infected branches when the pycnidia appear. In addition to

The pycnidia of Macrophoma leaf spot can grow on the lower or upper leaf surface of boxwood.

pruning out the fungus, the removal of branches will improve the air circulation through the plant which will help contain and eliminate the fungus. The fungus prefers a moist, cool, dark area which can be found in the centre of dense boxwood plants. The real secret of control is not to let the Macrophoma *leaf spot get started. The most effective preventative measure, annual thinning of the foliage, is far easier to perform than trying to restore a diseased boxwood.*

Volutella

Volutella buxi, *is a stem blight or canker found primarily on mature, thick* B. sempervirens *'Suffruticosa'. Its growth and development are especially severe in periods of high humidity. In moist weather, a mass of colourful and distinctive creamy and light pink to orange dust or fuzz-like growth is visible on the underside of the leaf and on branches. This stage is often overlooked because it forms in the most dense portions of the plant. The pink spore masses may not be visible under dry conditions. As the infection continues, the outer green leaves will become quickly and progressively discoloured, changing to a dark brown and then tan-colour. As the disease progresses, the entire branch will drop all of its leaves. The final stage results in the death of entire stem and attached branches.*

Volutella *will usually cause the soft tissue of the current year's growth to discolour black. If the plant is weak, the discolouration will extend well into the previous year's growth, producing a stem canker. A canker is formed from a wound or a dead, discoloured area that often sinks beneath the bark on the stem. On the trunk and larger branches, the healthy tissue immediately next to the canker may slightly increase in thickness and appear higher than the normal surface. Cankers will produce a crack on the surface of the bark that may be several inches in length. These cracks cause wilting and death to the parts of the branch beyond the canker.*

To avoid the initial infection, do not irrigate boxwood with any method that wets the foliage. Frequent rain or overhead watering encourages establishment of Volutella. Maintain a properly thinned boxwood to improve air circulation, and encourage rapid drying. Keep the boxwood in vigorous health by following good cultural practices. To control established infections, prune the diseased branch 6" to 12" (15 cm to 30 cm) below the affected tissue. This is best done during dry weather to prevent spreading the spores. Remove the diseased branches from the site.

Cylindrocladium

A relatively new disease is boxwood blight, known as Cylindrocladium *sp., a micro-fungus. First appearing in Europe in the mid-1990s, it infects the leaves, causing spots that lead to defoliation, and rapidly moves into stem tissue, leading to the death of smaller branches. Over a few weeks black streaks appear on the bark and the greyish fungus may be seen on the underside of the leaves. Heavy shearing resulting in dense foliage provides an ideal environment for this disease which can defoliate a mature plant in a matter of weeks. As with other boxwood fungal diseases, prevention by thinning overly-thick foliage is very effective.*

Decline

Finally, boxwood decline deserves mention. While the specific pathogen is a topic of much debate, Paecilomyces buxi *(formerly* Verticillium buxi*) is presumed responsible for boxwood decline. Decline is thought to be the result of fungi or nematodes that invade the root or crown portions of the boxwood that are culturally weak. There does appear to be a complex of several fungi, parasitic nematodes, and environmental and cultural factors associated with decline. Their specific interaction with each other and their association with the decline is not clearly understood. Decline is limited to B. sempervirens 'Suffruticosa'. The distribution of decline at one time extended from New York to North Carolina and the Appalachian Mountains. Numerous cases of boxwood*

Foliage bronzing created by stressful abiotic conditions see page 17

23

decline were reported in the 1970s, while today known incidents of boxwood decline are rare. There have been no reported cases of boxwood decline in Europe.

Boxwood in poor health are susceptible to boxwood decline. There is no tested, proven treatment for it. Initial infections can be avoided by keeping B. sempervirens 'Suffruticosa' culturally healthy. The deepest roots are affected first. As the disease progresses, the stem below the ground begins to turn brown. This will extend upward into branches, often in a random pattern. The above-ground symptoms take the form of small leaves that are brittle and yellow or red-coloured as well as characteristic browning of one branch or several branches. In severe cases, there is a sudden wilting of foliage or dieback of entire branches, resulting in the death of the boxwood. Improving cultural conditions, including soil drainage and thinning, has been suggested as the best control. Removal of the plant has often been necessary when the problem is serious.

Boxwood that are selected, placed, and maintained without considering their cultural needs are invitations for disease and disappointment. Culturally stressed boxwood can only weaken and become predisposed to disease and its associated problems. An intimate understanding of boxwood and the cultural environment necessary to foster healthy growth must be the primary concern to everyone who grows boxwood. Only then can boxwood exhibit their best characteristics and make their most effective contribution to the landscape.

Lynn R. Batdorf has been the Curator of the National Boxwood Collection at the United States National Arboretum in Washington, D.C. since 1977. He has been serving as the International Cultivar Registration Authority for Boxwood for the last 18 years and is an Honorary Life Member of both the European Boxwood and Topiary Society and the American Boxwood Society.

He has authored the popular book, **Boxwood Handbook: a Practical Guide to Knowing and Growing Boxwood** *and has published nearly 60 technical articles, whilst lecturing widely, on a variety of boxwood topics. In 2002 he participated in a month-long boxwood expedition to Azerbaijan and the Republic of Georgia.*

Batdorfl@usna.ars.usda.gov

RHS Update by Dr Beatrice Henricot

*L*eaf blight and stem infections in box are associated with
several fungi. One, Volutella buxi has been known for
a long time, although it has been little studied. It was
considered to be the main cause of leaf and twig blight on
box plants until the appearance of Cylindrocladium, which
currently causes great concern among box growers.

Cylindrocladium blight on Buxus has been recognised in
the UK since the mid-1990s. Cylindrocladium blight has
also been confirmed in Belgium, Ireland and New Zealand
and there are reports suggesting that it occurs in Italy,
France and Holland. The disease caused by Cylindrocladium
appears to cause more damage than Volutella, although
Volutella is frequently found on plants which have been
attacked by Cylindrocladium.

The number of cases recorded through the RHS advisory
service has been increasing since 1998 and the disease is
now widespread throughout the UK. The number of cases
usually peaks during the autumn months from September
to November. The symptoms of the disease are dark brown
spots on the leaves and black streaks on the stems. As a
result of infection, the plants defoliate and dieback ensues.

The fungus was isolated and initially identified as
Cylindrocladium scoparium. In order to classify this isolate
correctly, both traditional morphological techniques and DNA
sequence-based technology were used. The shape of the
vesicles and sequence data from three different regions of the
genome revealed that this fungus was in fact a new species.

The name C. buxicola has been accepted as its species
name. Interestingly, the genetic information did not reveal a
close relationship to any other described species of

Cylindrocladium. *This may be because this species has been introduced recently to Europe, where* Buxus *plants are widely grown, from a geographically isolated area where it evolved on one or more* Buxus spp.

To date, Cylindrocladium *blight has only been recorded on species of* Buxus *but the host range of this fungal species has not been fully established. The plants on which the disease has been recorded so far are* B. sempervirens', B. sempervirens 'Suffruticosa', B. sempervirens *'Variegata'.* B. sempervirens 'Suffruticosa Variegata', B. sempervirens 'Elegantissima', B. sempervirens *'Latifolia Maculata',* B. sinica var insularis *'Justin Brouwers',* B. microphylla var Japonica 'Morris Midget' and B. microphylla var Japonica 'National'. *Research is underway to determine if other* Buxus *species are susceptible to disease and preliminary results indicate that no* Buxus *species tested so far is immune to the disease.*

The RHS is also studying the infection biology of the fungus. The condition that particularly favours infection is high humidity. In dry conditions, the spores will abort quickly. This may be one reason why the Buxus *plants which have been worst affected are those with tightly packed leaves which encourage a humid microclimate. There are also studies looking at the survival of* C. buxicola *in the soil.*

So far, the fungus has been able to survive on decomposing leaf material for 17 months. Finally we are aiming to identify fungicides which would be effective in controlling this fungus, so that we can request the manufacturers to apply for product approval against box blight.

Dr. Henricot has a PhD from the University of Norwich, where she studied the pathogenicity of Cladosporium fulvum, a pathogen causing leaf mould on tomato. She studied for an MSc in Molecular Genetics at the University of Leicester and her first degree was in Agronomy at the Catholic University of Louvain of Belgium.

The European Boxwood and Topiary Society

*T*he European Boxwood and Topiary Society (EBTS) was formed in 1996 to bring together enthusiastic gardeners, botanists, growers, garden designers, landscape architects and garden historians. The EBTS aims to introduce new species and cultivars of boxwood, improve its cultivation and maintenance and explore topiary as an art form. It also has as objective the increase in knowledge, appreciation and science of boxwood and topiary and to make available up-to-date information on these aspects worldwide.

The Society meets for the weekend twice a year, once in Britain in early Summer and once in countries of Continental Europe in the Autumn. The programme of the British Summer meeting, held at an appropriate stately home, consists of the Annual General Meeting, followed by short lectures by botanists who are leaders in their field, renowned garden designers and landscape architects, or leading growers, all of whom EBTS is fortunate to count amongst its membership. Amongst the events organised there are demonstrations of boxwood cultivars and frame topiary, books and relevant products and a 'Meet the Experts' session where members can ask questions or seek help with their individual problems.

In addition the weekend includes visits to nearby gardens where topiary or boxwood is a particular feature.

The Continental European meeting consists of garden, nursery and château visits where the Society has access to gardens of importance, some of which are not open to the public. Each occasion offers members the chance to meet together in congenial surroundings and share their knowledge and experiences as well as learn new techniques.

For further information contact the Membership Secretary email: Lynda.hinton@classicfm.net

Gardens to Visit

*T*he list on the following pages includes gardens with box hedging, parterres and topiary. Also those with other topiary plantings such as yew and holly. Some may have both, others either yew or box and the list is by no means exhaustive. Many of the gardens are owned by the National Trust, some are owned privately but open on certain days during the year either under the National Gardens Scheme (NGS) or on a local Open Gardens Day. Others are open to groups only by prior appointment. Details of the NGS scheme can be found in the yellow NGS guides, available from local libraries, newsagents and bookshops. Hudson's Historic Houses and Gardens *is an excellent companion reference work for further details of the gardens in the UK listed here, as well as for other places of interest to the box and topiary enthusiast.*

If you are travelling without these guides it is always advisable to ring and check the opening times before setting out.

ENGLAND

BERKSHIRE

Dorney Court, Dorney,
nr. Windsor
01628 604638

BUCKINGHAMSHIRE

Ascott, Wing, nr. Leighton
Buzzard (Beds.)
01296 688242
Chenies Manor, Chenies, nr.
Chesham
01494 762888
Cliveden, Taplow, nr.
Maidenhead
01628 605069

CHESHIRE

Arley Hall, Arley, nr.
Northwich
01565 777353
Little Moreton Hall,
Congleton
01260 272018
Peover Hall, Over Peover, nr.
Knutsford
01565 632358
Tatton Park, Knutsford
01565 654822

CUMBRIA

Levens Hall, nr. Kendal
01359 560321

DERBYSHIRE

Chatsworth, Buxton
01246 582204
Elvaston Castle, Elvaston, nr.
Derby
01332 571342
Hardwick Hall, Doe Lea, nr.
Chesterfield
01246 850430
Melbourne Hall, Melbourne
01332 862502
Renishaw Hall,
nr. Chesterfield
01777 860755

DORSET

Athelhampton House,nr.
Dorchester
01305 848363
Cranborne Manor,
Cranborne,nr. Wimborne
01725 517248
Parnham House,
nr.Beaminster
01308 862204

ESSEX

Saling Hall, Saling, nr.
Gt.Braintree
01371 850243

GLOUCESTERSHIRE

Barnsley House, Barnsley,
nr.Cirencester
01285 740281
Hidcote Manor, nr.Chipping
Camden
01386 438333
Painswick Churchyard,
Painswick, nr.Stroud
Rodmarten Manor, nr.
Cirencester
01285 841253
Sudeley Castle, Winchcombe
nr. Cheltenham 01242
603197
Westbury Court Garden,
Westbury-upon-Severn
01452 760461

HAMPSHIRE

Houghton Lodge, nr.
Stockbridge
01264 810177
Mottisfont Abbey, Mottisfont,
nr. Romsey
01794 340757
Tudor House Museum, Bugle
St.
Southampton 01703 635904

HEREFORD &
WORCESTER

Hanbury Hall, nr. Droitwich
01527 8221214

HERTFORDSHIRE

Hatfield House, Hatfield
01707 262823

KENT

Doddington Place,
Doddington, nr. Sittingbourne
01795 886101
Goodnestone Park,
Goodnestone
01304 840107
Groombridge Place,
Groombridge
01892 863999
Hall Place, Bexley
01322 526574
Hever Castle, nr. Edenbridge
01732 865224
Penshurst Place. Penshurst
01892 870307
Sissinghurst Castle,
nr. Cranbrook
01580 715330
Squerryes Court, Westerham
01959 562345

LONDON

Chiswick House, Burlington
Lane, W4
0208 955 0508
Museum of Garden History,
Palace Rd.
Lambeth, SE1
0207 261 1891

NORFOLK

Blickling Hall, nr. Aylsham
01263 733084
Felbrigg Hall, nr. Cromer
01263 837444

NORTHAMPTONSHIRE

Coton Manor, Guilsborough
01604 740219
Holdenby House, Holdenby
01604 770074

NORTHUMBERLAND

Herterton House, nr. Cambo
(Morpeth) 01670 774278
Seaton Delaval Hall, Seaton
Sluice 0191 237 3040

OXFORDSHIRE

Beckley Park, Beckley
Blenheim Palace, Woodstock
01993 811091

RUTLAND

Clipsham Hall Avenue,
Clipsham

SOMERSET

Claverton Manor, (The
American Museum) Bath
01225 460503
Tintinhull Garden, Tintinhull,
Yeovil
01935 822545

STAFFORDSHIRE

Biddulph Grange Garden,
Biddulph
01782 517999

SUFFOLK

Helmingham Hall,
Helmingham
01473 890363

SURREY

Goddards. Abinger Common,
Dorking
01306 730871
Ham House, Ham, nr.
Richmond
0208 940 1950
Hampton Court Palace,
Hampton Wick
0208 781 9500

SUSSEX EAST

Brickwall House, Northiam
01797 223329
Great Dixter, Northiam
01797 252878

SUSSEX WEST

Fishbourne Roman Palace
01243 785859
Nymans Gardens, Handcross
01444 400321
West Dean Gardens, West
Dean 01243 811301

WILTSHIRE

Bowood House, nr. Calne
01249 812102
Heale Garden, Woodford
01722 782504
Heywood House Lodge,
Heywood
Longleat House, nr.
Warminster
01985 844400

YORKSHIRE

Harewood House, Harewood
0113 288 6331

SCOTLAND

GRAMPIAN

Crathes Castle, Banchory
01330 844525
Hazelhead Park, nr. Aberdeen
Pitmedden Garden, Ellon, nr.
Aberdeen
01651 842352

PERTHSHIRE

Drummond Castle, Crieff
01764 681257

Roxburghshire
Floors Castle, Kelso
01573 223333

WALES

CLWYD

Chirk Castle, Chirk
01691 777701
Erdigg, nr. Wrexham
01978 355314

GWYNEDD

Plas-in-Rhiw, Rhiw, nr.
Pwllheli

POWYS

Powis Castle, nr. Welshpool
01938 554338

EIRE

CO. DOWN

Mount Stewart, nr.
Newtonnards
028 4278 8387

CO. OFFALY

Birr Castle Demesne, Birr
+353 509 20336

Co. Wicklow

Powerscourt Estate,
Enniskerry
353 1679 4144

The Collectors' Series of Trees

Are you collecting… ?

"… and a very charming book it is…"
Roy Lancaster, on MONKEY PUZZLE

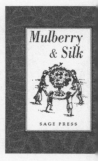

TREES STIR passions in us all, whether from climbing them in our youth or just from their natural beauty, we all feel a deep affinity with these majestic, timeless, immobile forms.

How better to deepen our love for trees than a series of books celebrating this unique heritage, the amusing and well-balanced text complimented by Chris Monk's delightfully quirky illustrations.

In the same series

Ash
Box
Cedar of Lebanon
Fig
Hawthorn
Holly
Monkey Puzzle
Mulberry
Oak
Sitka Spruce
Yew

Future Titles

Black Poplar
Wild Service Tree
Willow for Basketmakers

Also available

The Puzzle Puzzle Jigsaw

If you enjoyed this title and would like to buy any
of the above titles or require further information
please contact

SAGE PRESS
PO Box № 1, Rye, East Sussex TN36 6HN.
e-mail: sagepress.bm@btinternet.com
www.sagepress.co.uk